The Glorious Revolution: The
England by William of Orange

By Charles River Editors

A depiction of William of Orange boarding a ship for England

About Charles River Editors

Introduction

A depiction of William of Orange landing in England

The Glorious Revolution

"We have great reason to believe, we shall be every day in a worse condition than we are, and less able to defend ourselves, and therefore we do earnestly wish we might be so happy as to find a remedy before it be too late for us to contribute to our own deliverance ... the people are so generally dissatisfied with the present conduct of the government, in relation to their religion, liberties and properties (all which have been greatly invaded), and they are in such expectation of their prospects being daily worse, that your Highness may be assured, there are nineteen parts of twenty of the people throughout the kingdom, who are desirous of a change; and who, we believe, would willingly contribute to it, if they had such a protection to countenance their rising, as would secure them from being destroyed. – Excerpt from the invitation by The Seven to William of Orange to become monarch

17th century Europe, particularly its latter years, is often hailed as the beginning of the Enlightenment as nations across the continent experienced a surge in innovation and scientific progress, a period also commonly referred to as the Age of Reason. There was English natural philosopher, Francis Bacon, whose book *Novum Organum* challenged Aristotelian philosophy and stressed the significance of inductive reasoning. Bacon's ideas, which emphasized observation and the implementation of various premises to form conclusions, was later referenced by famed French mathematician René Descartes.

Bacon

This illustrious age also inspired a brilliant burst in art and creativity. Progressive but hot button topics were greeted with resounding choruses of approval. One of these forward-thinkers was renowned English philosopher, John Locke, one of the forefathers of political liberalism. Locke was a staunch believer in the abolishment of the Divine Right of Kings, which was the God-given right for monarchs to rule over a nation. This was an archaic system wherein rebellion was considered the worst of all political crimes, and a system that not only made tyranny much more probable but condoned it. Locke was opposed to the doctrine of papal infallibility, which essentially rendered the pope faultless when it came to his teachings about religion and morals, though this has since been disputed by the modern Catholic Church. This was one of the driving points of his opposition towards an English Catholic king. Locke, a follower of Thomas Hobbes, another respected player in the field, echoed the idea that men are intrinsically free and independent souls, born with no obligation or duty to one another, and should be able to pursue whatever interest they so pleased.

Locke

These radical ideas were bordering on blasphemous, but it was, perhaps, in a sense, necessary. The Enlightenment had been awakened by the European Age of Discovery, a transformative era that succeeded the Medieval Years of Yore, but the continent was also a seedbed of insurrection, holy wars, and volatility. People were growing weary of the unpredictable system of monarchy, a post that was inherited only by members of an exclusive bloodline or connection, one that often muted the voices of the people.

Time and time again, grossly incompetent and seemingly diabolic rulers had come to power through the rigged regal system. For starters, there was John, King of England, the real-life inspiration of the evil and infantile lion in the beloved Disney animation *Robin Hood*, a retelling of the tale with anthropomorphic animals. King John was said to have been power-hungry but politically feckless, and a sadistic soul who delighted in cruel and inhumane torture. The king did away with nearly everyone that had slighted him, including his own nephew, his political rival. This was a man whose reputation was so horrid, chroniclers and academics have summed him up as an "absolute rotter."

Then, there was Queen Mary I of England, who earned herself the less-than-pleasant moniker of "Bloody Mary." While in power, Mary vowed to restore papal authority and revert England to Catholicism, placing the bullseye on Protestants. Laws against heresy made a bloody comeback, which saw hundreds of Protestants dragged to the stakes. Naturally, the oppressed began to revolt. Bands of insurgents flooded the city streets, torching city buildings and governmental establishments. Ambitious assassination plots were hatched across the land as conspirators conjured up planned poisonings, midnight sneak attacks, and other desperate ways to dispose of the tyrants.

However, an uprising of a completely different nature would soon unfold on English soil – the Glorious Revolution, an intriguing story of a power war exacerbated by ruthless ambition, under-the-table plotting, and the treachery of familial betrayal. In 1678, a sinister scheme to assassinate King Charles II was unearthed, sending the public into a frenzy of mass panic. Fingers were pointed at the Catholics, who had been accused of concocting the elaborate conspiracy, and this very event would intensify the white-hot flames of the Anti-Catholic hysteria that was already running unchecked within the nation. 7 years later, the openly Catholic King James II rose to the throne, and needless to say, the largely Protestant public was anything but pleased. As the people slowly turned against him, the king's daughter, Mary, and her husband, William of Orange, watched across the English Channel from a distance. The people were begging for change in a broken system, and something drastic had to and would be done.

The Glorious Revolution: The History of the Overthrow of King James II of England by William of Orange explores the story of an English kingdom in turmoil, and how one king's overly ambitious quest led to his undoing. It also tells the story of how the aspiring monarchs achieved their prize in this "Bloodless Revolution" with a political game of cat and mouse, assisted along the way by secret plotting, persistence, and betrayal in order to forever change the course of history. Along with pictures depicting important people, places, and events, you will learn about the Glorious Revolution like never before.

James the Catholic

"'Twas the divine Providence that drove me early out of my native country, and 'twas the same Providence ordered it so that I past most of the 12 years I was abroad in Catholic kingdoms, by which means I came to know what their religion was." – King James II

On October 14, 1633, the royal chambers of St. James's Palace erupted with the first cries of the royal newborn. The baby boy was to be named after his grandfather, and was soon introduced to the English public as James II. Queen Henrietta Maria, exalted but exhausted, held her baby in her arms, cooing lovingly at her creation. The nagging pain of the miscarriage she had suffered just 4 years ago, where she had lost her son, Charles James, slowly ebbed, and her heart swelled with joy and sweet relief. With her husband, England's very own King Charles I, she would have 6 more surviving children: Charles II; Henrietta; Mary, Princess Royal; Anne; Henry Stuart, Duke of Gloucester; and Elizabeth Stuart.

Tony Hisgett's picture of the St. James's Palace

Young James II with his father, Charles I of England

A few months after James was born, he was baptized by William Laud, the Anglican Archbishop of Canterbury. From an early age, James and his older brother, Charles II, were given daily lessons by a hand-picked selection of the nation's finest private tutors. On James's 3rd birthday, he was appointed the honorary title of Lord High Admiral, but would later take up the title as an adult. At age 11, young James was officially made the Duke of York.

Having grown up in the opulently decorated red-bricked towers and lavish courtyards of the Palace, it was safe to say that James was far more blessed than most when it came to his childhood. Unfortunately, that smooth life of luxury came skidding to a halt. In 1642, the "Roundheads" (Parliamentarian rebels against King Charles I) and the "Cavaliers" (monarchists) faced off in a violent chain of armed conflicts and political upheavals that lasted 9 years, otherwise known as the English Civil War. English Protestants had never been too keen on the king, who they held a grudge against for marrying the Catholic Henrietta Maria, as well as his retaliatory disbanding of Parliament on multiple occasions.

During the siege of Oxford in 1646, Parliamentarian leaders placed the Duke of York under house arrest. There he remained for 2 years, until royalist colonel Joseph Bampfield snuck into St. James's Palace. There, James donned a wig and a dress and was smuggled out of the palace and into the Hague in Netherlands.

16-year-old James was clocked with a second blow of terrible news; his father had been captured by Parliamentarians and tried in high court, where he was found guilty of treason. In early 1649, the king was beheaded. James's brother, Charles II, was declared king by the

Cavaliers, but would fail to get his hands on the English crown until later. For the meantime, he fled to France.

Charles II of England

James also sought refuge in France, and it was there that he had his first taste of the battlefield when he joined the French army, but he would later cross over to the Spanish side in 1656. When he joined the Spanish army, he struck up a close friendship with a pair of Irish Catholic brothers. By 1660, the conflicts had simmered down, and his brother was formally crowned the king of England.

When James returned home that year, eyebrows around England shot up as the king's brother announced his engagement to Anne Hyde. People began to whisper about the choice since she was nothing more than a commoner, the simple daughter of Charles's chief minister. No one approved of the peculiar pairing, and for weeks, their loved ones badgered them, urging them not to proceed with the wedding. Queen Henrietta's skin crawled with the idea of her son marrying "beneath him." Even Anne Hyde's own father attempted to talk his daughter out of the marriage.

Nevertheless, in early September of that year, the lovebirds eloped. Anne Hyde gave birth to their first son, Charles, less than 60 days later, but he, along with 5 of his future siblings, never made it past their 2nd birthdays. Only 2 of their daughters would survive – Mary, and a younger sister who shared the same name with their mother, Anne.

Anne Hyde

In spite of his sacred vows, historians have often hinted at James's wandering eye, painting the philanderer as "the most unguarded ogler of the time." Like many other monarchs, he more than tainted the sanctity of marriage with his side collection of mistresses. James had a particular thing for "plain," slender Catholic maidens in their teens, including Arabella Churchill, Catherine Sedley, and 9 other young ladies.

Before Anne Hyde's death in 1671, James and his wife began to stray from their Anglican faith, and explored the Catholic Church. In 1669, 36-year-old James was said to have taken communion in a Roman Catholic Church, though this was kept under wraps. He carried on the Anglican facade for a few more years, attending Anglican services and mingling with Anglicans and Protestants, including John Churchill, the brother of one of his mistresses.

In 1672, King Charles II signed the Royal Declaration of Indulgence, otherwise known as the "Declaration for Liberty of Conscience." This suspended all penalties targeted at those outside the Protestant Church of England and granted Catholics and other non-Protestants the right to worship freely. This religious freedom was short-lived, however, as members of Parliament criticized their new king and named him a Catholic sympathizer. The horrendous fate of his father still fresh on his mind, Charles canceled the declaration the next year.

In 1673, Parliament established the Test Act of 1673, and present and aspiring members of office and the military were now required to swear an oath to the monarch and the Protestant Church of England. In the same breath, they were to denounce the Catholic doctrine of transubstantiation, which was the transformation of bread and wine to the real body and blood of Christ during the sacrament of the Eucharist, which the English Protestants branded "superstitious and idolatrous." That same year, James refused this oath and stepped down from his post as Lord High Admiral. There were gasps from every corner of the country; the king's own brother, the Duke of York, was a Catholic. The humiliated king was furious, demanding that his nieces, 11-year-old Mary and 8-year-old Anne, follow tradition and be raised as Protestants. "Under fear of their being taken away from him altogether," James reluctantly agreed. When asked about his change of heart, James held up his chin and replied, "The divisions among Protestants and the necessity of an infallible judge to decide controversies, together with some promises which Christ made to his church in general...there being no person that pretends to infallibility but the Bishop of Rome."

Later that year, Charles found himself exasperated again when James became engaged to an Italian princess, the Catholic Mary of Modena. He was hopelessly smitten with the stunning princess, described as a milk-skinned beauty with jet-black hair and eyes "so full of light and sweetness." This beauty had also come with brains, as the young girl could write in both Latin and French, and she had great interest and talent in music and art. Charles grumbled about it, but ultimately he gave his brother and sister-in-law-to-be his blessings. In late September of 1673, James tied the knot once more with his new 15-year-old bride.

Yet again, these wedding bells brought nothing but obligatory rounds of halfhearted congratulations. Some kept a vigilant eye on the new Duchess of York, who they believed was a spy or a secret agent of sorts that had been dispatched by the pope himself. In fact, the infamous Popish Plot that would arise 5 years later only further stirred the simmering pot.

Mary of Modena

William Who?

"I cannot approve of monarchs who want to rule over the conscience of the people, and take away their freedom of choice and religion." – William the Silent, great-grandfather of William III

1677 proved to be a particularly difficult year for James, one that came with a karmic twist. King Charles II arranged for the marriage between James's favorite daughter, 15-year-old Mary, and 27-year-old Protestant, William III. As rough as it was for James, it was said to have been worse for young Mary. Apart from being forced to take part in a marriage that the teenager had never asked for, William III was her first cousin, the son of James's sister Mary, Princess Royal. Mary was said to have burst into tears at the first sight of her unattractive cousin, a feeble, waxy-faced man with beady eyes, a bulky nose, and a crooked back. Her younger sister, Anne, stood by her sobbing sister's side, rather unkindly comparing her new brother-in-law to Prince Calibos (a mythological but grotesque swamp creature that had been cursed with deformity by the Greek god Zeus).

Mary

William III of Orange

As an interesting side note, some historians claim that Mary was a lesbian. From the age of 9 to 15, Mary wrote "passionate" letters with alleged romantic undertones to an older girl she idolized, Frances Apsley. Later, Apsley would also be Mary's maid of honor. Having said that, most historians dismiss the claim as rubbish. Others have also questioned the true nature of Anne's true sexuality.

James was said to have initially objected to the Protestant marriage, but after a bit of arm-twisting from his brother and other influential members of Parliament, the Duke of York conceded. Needless to say, the wedding, which took place in early November of that year, was anything but pretty. Mary's wedding dress was stained with the tears teeming down her face as she stood by the visibly uncomfortable William, while a poker-faced but nervous James watched the ceremony. King Charles was supposedly the only one in genuinely good spirits, all smiles as he cracked jokes back and forth, hoping to ease the tension. Unbeknownst to those present, the fidgety, unassuming groom would one day make a name for himself, in ways no one could have ever imagined.

William III of Orange was born in the Hague on November 4, 1650. While in his mother's womb, his father, William II, Prince of Orange and the stadtholder of the Netherlands, fell ill with smallpox and lost the battle against the debilitating disease. One week later, William II's grieving wife, Mary, went into labor, garbed from head to toe in soulless black. At age 9, young

William would lose his mother to the same wretched disease.

William II of Orange

William III had always been a sickly child, remembered by those in his time as a gaunt, asthmatic tyke born with a curved spine that gave him a faint hunchback. That said, William was an exceptionally bright child, and even with his physical shortcomings – or perhaps, as a product of them – the shrewd and patient William was determined to achieve greatness. Brothers Jan and Cornelius De Witt had assumed power of stadtholder after his father's death, and William was willing to go to any lengths to reclaim that title.

In an early display of William's cunning and persistence, he rolled up his sleeves and took advantage of the education at his disposal. With the help of Calvinist tutors, William learned the ins and outs of history, politics, and war. Along the way, he would not only pick up but master 4 different languages.

In 1672, the persistence of William and the Orangist party paid off. The public criticized the De Witt brothers for their failure to protect Flanders from French King Louis XIV's invading forces, and the pair were soon out of their post. In July that year, 22-year-old William was promoted from captain general to stadtholder, and the next month, the De Witt brothers were murdered by an angry mob.

Louis XIV

William's reign as stadtholder would be turbulent, particularly during the Dutch Wars from 1672 to 1678. He suffered great wins and devastating losses, and at times he squared off against armies of men 5 times his size, but William persevered. Throughout these years, he also managed to form close bonds with the leaders of Denmark, Brandenburg, and Spain. He would even experience a near brush with death when he was diagnosed with smallpox, made worse by a badly infected arm wound, but unlike his parents, he won that battle.

Though William and Mary's marriage had appeared doomed from the get-go, the pair would eventually grow to not only respect but love one another. This was not just a relationship based on an unlikely romance, it was a partnership that thrived on their shared drive for power and status. Soon, this dynamic power couple would ever so quietly paddle up to the surface and blow everyone out of the water.

As fate would have it, James was right to have second thoughts about the marriage after all.

Broken Promises

"If by the mere force of numbers a majority should deprive a minority of any clearly written constitutional right, it might, in a moral point of view, justify revolution." – President Abraham Lincoln, "First Inaugural Address"

Unfortunately for James, his daughter's Protestant marriage would pale in comparison to what was in store for him. Other than the hysteria that had been charged by the Popish Plot a year after William and Mary exchanged their vows, which further turned the Protestant public against the Catholics, James became the subject of an exclusion campaign. Panic began to rise on the Protestant side when after 16 years of marriage, King Charles II, and his wife, Catherine of Braganza, bore no live children. While Charles reportedly had 12 illegitimate children by a range of voluptuous mistresses, some of them sons, none of these bastard sons would ever have a chance at the throne, and the Protestants would not accept a Catholic king on the throne in the form of James should something happen to Charles.

Thus, the Earl of Shaftesbury, an ex-government minister and one of the most vocal opponents of the Catholic Church, fought to have James personally excluded from the throne in a formal Exclusion Bill. James took this up with his brother. He lamented, "Matters were come to such a head that the monarchy must be either more absolute or quite abolished."

In 1679, as Parliament threatened to pass the Exclusion Bill, the king took a stand. For the sake of his brother, he dissolved Parliament. 2 more parties of Parliament were formed in the next 2 years, but these were again knocked down at the slightest mention of the hotly contested Exclusion Bill. The quarreling sides split by the messy exclusion dilemma would help give rise to 2 political parties – the "Tories," who sided with the monarch in opposing the bill, and the "Whigs," the Parliamentarian rebels who supported it.

This Exclusion Bill would never be passed, but a discouraged James, hoping to shun the dreaded spotlight, retired to a lesser governmental post and made himself scarce. James later left for Brussels and would only return to England during dire times, including when his brother fell ill. Eventually, the Catholic panic began to dissipate, but there remained a perpetual rift between James and the Protestant Parliament.

As things were playing out around this time, on October 12, 1678, Sir Edmund Berry Godfrey, an esteemed Justice of the Peace, was brutally murdered. Godfrey was found face-down and sprawled out in a ditch, his own sword thrust deep into his lifeless corpse. Investigators later examined the battered body and reported he had a number of bruises and a strange, circular mark around his neck that indicated strangulation. Oddly, the bloodless wound of his sword suggested that it had been plunged into him hours after his death. Even more curious, there were no signs of a struggle near the crime scene, and though his body had been in the ditch for over 96 hours, his leather belt-wallet was still plump with cash and the winking rings on his fingers untouched. This was not a robbery gone wrong; there was clearly more to the case than met the eye.

Godfrey

A series of men would eventually be rounded up to pay for the crime. A day before Christmas, a Catholic servant named Miles Prance confessed to being one of the alleged conspirators, and he coughed up the names of the supposed masterminds: 3 Catholic priests. All 3 men of the cloth were apparently present during the murder, but those with actual blood on their hands were another trio of working men named Henry Berry, Robert Green, and Lawrence Hill. The 3 men were arrested and hanged in Primrose Hill in February of 1679.

This startling event shook the already hysterical masses. Just a month before the murder, a man by the name of Titus Oates had been summoned by the deceased to swear an oath on his testimony before it was presented to the king. The grim-faced magistrate listened as Oates relayed a terrible plot woven together by a rogue band of rebellious Catholics which had been drawn up during a secret Jesuit meeting in the White Horse Tavern of London. According to Oates, these rebels planned to assassinate King Charles II and replace him with his Catholic brother, James II. Oates recounted convincing details of possible methods that had made an appearance on the drawing board. One rebel suggested employing Irish mercenaries to stab the king in his slumber. One suggested an ambush by armed Jesuit soldiers. Another proposed a more subtle tactic by poisoning the monarch with the aid of the Queen's own personal physician.

Oates' sensational accusations only fueled the Catholic resentment that was already festering within the English community. The idea of colluding Catholics conniving to take over England was was not difficult to swallow; just 12 years before, in early September of 1666, a relentless fire was sparked in the home of King Charles' baker and would soon spread throughout London, running wild for 4 days before the fire was finally extinguished by authorities. By then, 80% of the city lay in smoldering ruins. The blame was passed around until it ultimately landed on the Catholics, who were accused of an act of religious terrorism. Despite the fact that authorities openly disproved this theory, the animosity the public had towards the Catholics intensified.

Oates would tell the story of the great plot to anyone who would listen. Soon, that was exactly what they did. For 3 years, the public soaked up these stories, and at least 15 men would be arrested and executed as a result of Oates' accusations. It was only when magistrates and the king himself began to grill Oates that authorities began to notice the holes and various inconsistencies in his stories. Eventually, Oates' house of cards came crashing down, and the gobsmacked public learned that no such plot had ever existed. The details of Oates' background check were published for the masses; Oates was a disgraced turncoat who had once belonged to the Catholic Church, but was expelled for "drunken blasphemy." Oates later became the chaplain for a royal navy ship, but he was once more dismissed for the crime of sodomy.

These stories had been nothing but the product of a vengeful madman's imagination. Years later, a judge declared many of these executed men posthumously innocent. This controversial event is now immortalized as the Popish Plot of 1678. While the muddied name of Titus Oates would never wash off, the damage had already been done. The largely Protestant public simply did not trust the Catholic Church.

Oates

The Popish Plot might have been purely fictitious, but things were about to get very real. In 1682, when the possibility of a Catholic king was soon to become a reality, anti-monarch extremists started to grow restless. The most devout partakers of the cause decided that something had to be done, and they began to conduct secret meetings to discuss their next move. Among these rebels were its leader, James Scott, the Duke of Monmouth and the illegitimate son of King Charles II; Lords Essex and William Russell; Sir Algernon Sydney; and Archibald Campbell, the Earl of Argyll. After the initial brainstorming session, the extremists had come to a consensus; the only way to ensure a future for Protestant England would be to kill the king and his proud Catholic brother, the Duke of York, then replace the monarch with James Scott, the Duke of Monmouth. One plotter suggested they shoot them from Bow Steeple, now known as the St. Mary-le-Bow Church. Another suggested that they make their move on Charles and James at St. James Park. Someone else proposed pouncing on the pair during a boat ride on the River Thames.

The Duke of Monmouth

Finally, a republican named Richard Rumbold cleared his throat, making himself heard. He offered his home, the Rye House, as their base, located just 18 miles outside of London. The well-to-do Civil War veteran lived in a handsome, fortified medieval mansion that was guarded by a moat. Eyes around the room brightened at once, and it was soon decided. Blueprints of the scheme were drawn. The attackers were to hide in the Rye House, where they would lie in wait. When an oblivious Charles and James returned from the horse races in Newmarket, the attackers would then leap out and lunge at them, slaying them on the spot. The plans were so detailed that nicknames were assigned to their targets. The sun-kissed Charles was named "Blackbird," and the fair-complexioned James was "Goldfinch."

The date of the assassination was planned for the 1st of April, 1683, but an unexpected turn of events would derail the entire mission. That afternoon, a major fire broke out in Newmarket, consuming half the city. The races were canceled, and the royal brothers returned to London early, completely unaware of how close they came to their deaths. 2 months later, a man named Josiah Keeling snitched on his conspirators, and the plot was made public. Over 2 dozen men were arrested for their involvement in the plot, and 12 would meet their grisly deaths – public executions where the men were hanged, drawn, and quartered. Another 2 were sentenced to death but would later be pardoned. At least 1 man suffered cruel and unusual punishment, and another committed suicide. 25 more were imprisoned, implicated, and fled into exile. Among the implicated was the Duke of Monmouth, but he would be pardoned and later moved to the Dutch Republic, where he lived for the time being. The nefarious failed scheme is now known as the "Rye House Plot."

By the 1680s, Catholicism had also begun to leave a bad taste in the mouths of the neighboring French people. In 1685, King Louis XIV rescinded the Edict of Nantes. The edict, which had been established by King Henry IV of France about a century prior, granted substantial rights and promoted religious tolerance to all men in the country, including the Calvinist Protestants. Louis, a known advocate for the Divine Right of Kings, declared Catholicism the dominant religion of France, and in doing so, he banned the practicing of all other religions, and set out on a mission to pluck the heretics out of the population. At the same time, he hounded the Protestants and forced them to convert with his policy of "dragonnades." Under this policy, special troops accosted and intimidated known Protestant families until they switched teams, or fled their homes.

In the months that followed, thousands of disheartened Protestants packed up their belongings and set out to search for greener pastures, so much so that by the early months of 1686, only an estimated 2,000 Protestants were left in France. Protestant defectors were soon scattered across Europe, and word about the wicked dangers of a Catholic tyranny had taken a life of its own. This was a fate that Protestants across the continent vowed to avoid at all costs.

On February 6, 1685, the 54-year-old King Charles II suffered a fatal apoplectic fit and passed away. With that, his younger brother James II was called upon to fill the vacant seat of the throne. The date of the coronation was set for 2 months later, on April 23rd, the Feast Day of St. George, England's patron saint.

And what a stupendous celebration it was. To commemorate the event, genealogist Francis Sandford was tasked with recording every last detail of the special day, from full descriptions of every scheduled event to intricate diagrams and drawings. The day kicked off with a procession from Westminster Hall to the Collegiate Church of St. Peter. Cheering crowds gathered in the streets to witness the momentous occasion, whistling and toasting their new king. A glowing James, along with the soon-to-be queen, Mary of Modena, waved at the sea of ruddy faces around them as trumpeters marched alongside them, the royals dressed in the finest robes made of purple velvet. The king's crown was breathtaking, crafted with velvet in a complementary shade of violet, studded with glittering diamonds and jewels, and topped off with a bedazzled crown ornament. The beautiful ceremony ended with a serenade from the heavenly voices of the choir, saluting the king with a Henry Purcell original, "My Heart is Inditing."

At 5:00 p.m., after a 5-hour long coronation ceremony, the new king and queen retired to Westminster Hall for a fabulous feast. The royals and their honored guests were seated around freshly polished tables boasting a jaw-dropping menu selection. The King and Queen themselves gorged on a total of 175 dishes, with 145 platters served as an appetizer course, and 30 dishes of hot meats in the following. A total of 1,445 dishes were served in the banquet hall that day, including "pistachio cream in glasses," "bolonia [sic] sausages," "pickled oysters," and "cold puffins." Every member of nobility had a servant hovering behind them, ready to cater to their every need. The celebratory fireworks, which were scheduled to be set alight over the picturesque view of the Thames River, was postponed to the following day.

As elaborately grand as the coronation was, the day seemed to be rife with bad omens. First, one of the canopy posts snapped, nearly crushing the king in the abbey. The crown, which had been exclusively minted for James II, did not fit him properly and nearly slipped off when it was placed on his head. The people whispered when the new king broke tradition by refusing the Anglican rite of communion, a featured event in all coronations before him.

The fireworks display was as impressive as it was disastrous, and a number of witnesses wrote about the catastrophe. Some of the rockets misfired, which prompted several boats to flip over in the chaos. What unfurled was a scene "so dreadful, that several spectators leaped into the river, choosing rather to be drowned than to be burned." At a nearby stable, spooked horses ran amok, leaving at least one coachman severely injured.

When James ascended to the throne in 1685, it appeared that he had hoped for a peaceful beginning. Bearing the sensitive religious tensions in his new country, James declared, "I shall make it my endeavor to preserve the government in Church and State as it is by law established. For a moment, Parliament and the Protestant public breathed easy.

One of James's first orders of business was to completely reconfigure the system. Top military and government officials were shuffled around and replaced with those known to be devout Catholics. Judges who did not concur with him were quickly booted out of the bench and substituted with justices who sided with his policies.

A brand new Parliament was set in place, each member a known James supporter. He created the Commission for Ecclesiastical Causes, devoted to punishing Anglican and Protestant clergymen who have either wronged him, or have refused to spread the Catholic word. Distinguished universities, including Christ Church and University College in Oxford, were now required by law to accept Catholic and other non-Protestant students. More eyes bulged when the king began to allow Catholics to hold important positions in university boards. The public was infuriated, but James was only warming up.

Shortly after James II rose to the throne, his reign was disrupted by 2 rebellions. The Duke of Monmouth had struck again, hungry for the crown. This time, Monmouth collaborated with another one of the alleged conspirators of the Rye House Plot, the Earl of Argyll. A third name is often associated as the great "plotter" of this new scheme: Robert Ferguson, a Scottish Presbyterian minister and the Duke's number one fan.

While in Holland, the duke and the earl had begun a public recruitment, assembling their army of riotous rebels, open to both men and women. The duke was able to attract a small, but feisty group of jaded farm workers, artisans, and other societal nonconformists, whereas the earl succeeded in collecting approximately 300 men for his campaign, known as the Campbells. Their new plan was set in motion – the earl was to take care of the royal forces based in Scotland, while the duke would deal with those in London. It must be noted that William of Orange was said to have been fully aware of the recruitment, but chose to turn a blind eye.

In early June, the earl and his Campbells crossed the seas to Scotland. There, the band quickly realized they had underestimated the size of the king's forces, and the mission was promptly cut short. On the 18th of that month, the earl was seized in the small Scottish village of Inchinnan. He was thrown into a prison in Edinburgh and was later sentenced to death. It was said that the smiling earl had taken his sentencing in stride. In fact, he had taken it so well, that he was found "sleeping soundly" by an official who had come expecting to drag him kicking and screaming to his death. He even bore these comforting words to his stepdaughter: "What shall I say in this great day of the Lord, wherein, in the midst of a cloud, I find a fair sunshine. I can wish no more for you...that the Lord may comfort you and shine upon you as he doth upon me, and give you that same sense of His love in staying in the world, as I have in going out of it."

Handling the Duke of Monmouth's forces was not as easy. The determined duke had pawned off many of his belongings for the occasion, using the funds to purchase ship, weaponry, and other necessary equipment for battle. His supportive wife and family pitched in with jewelry and other valuables of their own, providing him with extra funding. On the 11th of June, the duke proclaimed himself king in Lyme Regis, a charming coastal town in West England. Though the duke had only landed with just 1000 or so men, along with 3 small ships, 4 modest field guns, and just under 1,500 muskets, his band of rebels were less eager to surrender.

As luck would have it, James had been alerted of the duke's plans beforehand. The duke and his men were later easily defeated in the Battle of Sedgemoor. The duke was captured, taken to the Tower of London in mid-July, and had his head lopped off by the executioner, Jack Ketch. A thousand of these rebels were gathered and put on the hot seat in a series of trials known as the Bloody Assizes, which was overseen by 5 judges. 250 of these rebels were executed. One of the most controversial names among the sentenced was "gentlewoman" Dame Alice Lisle, who was found guilty and sent to burn at the stakes. As for the rest of the rebels, they were shipped off to the West Indies, where they were damned to live a life of "indentured servitude."

Perhaps as expected, James sought out to strengthen his defenses, amping up security for future rebellions that he knew was certain to come, and even after the early threats had petered out, he refused to dissolve his army. This immediately sent alarm bells ringing across the country. Doing so was strictly breaking code, as it was expected of rulers to disband armies during peacetime. Instead, James generated a "peacetime standing army" inspired by the French King Louis XIV.

Uniforms were introduced, weapons were upgraded, the required training now more extensive and hardcore, and a fixed rank system was set in place. 9 new infantry regiments (foot soldiers) and 7 cavalries (soldiers on horseback) were formed, and stationed all over England. A Catholic-run army was also raised in Ireland.

Naturally, this only worsened the already intense fear and rampant resentment against Catholics. Many raised a stink about it, fearing that the king would one day use this very army on his own subjects. More foreheads puckered when a few bad apples in the form of unruly soldiers began to stir up trouble and butt heads with the locals.

Apart from expanding the royal army, James disturbed the balance even more by adding a private council, consisting of all Catholic ministers. The Protestant public accused him of rubbing his Catholic faith in their faces. The king made no effort to conceal the Catholic masses held in the royal palace every week. It was against Parliament law for other religions to worship in public, but more Catholics began to step out of the dark, something the king encouraged heartily. James welcomed European Catholic missionaries into his land with open arms. Catholic chapels, schools, books, bibles, and other forms of media began to crop up all over England.

To the English Protestants, the most flagrant of these red flags were the king's continuous attempts to tackle traditional law. Week after week, James stood before Parliament, attempting to repeal the Test Acts, as well as all criminal laws that victimized Catholic and Protestant dissenters. When Parliament wagged their heads, rejecting his proposals, James ripped a page out of his brother's book and scrapped Parliament altogether.

James knew that he was treading on thin ice, and was quickly losing what few comrades he had. That same year, in 1686, the king met with the Quaker and founder of the Province of Pennsylvania, William Penn. A pact was formed between James, Penn, and other Protestant nonconformists, with all parties agreeing to provide support for one another to help ensure a future tolerant of all religions.

To the Protestants, the most problematic of the king's unremitting changes was the royal document he republished on April 4, 1688: The Declaration of Indulgence. The document aimed to negate all discriminatory laws on religion, and focused on 3 areas of change. First, all laws that penalized those of other religions who refused to attend or rejected communion rites from the Church of England were abolished. Second, people of all faiths were now allowed to worship in private houses or chapels. Third, the Test Acts would be canceled. No longer would those looking to advance in the government or military required to take various oaths outside of their preferred religion. These new laws applied to Protestants, Catholics, Jews, Muslims, Unitarians, and other nonconformists, including atheists. During a tour to promote this declaration of universal religious toleration, James stated, "...[S]uppose...there should be a law made that all black men should be imprisoned, it would be unreasonable and we had as little reason to quarrel with other men for being of different opinions as for being of different complexions."

The issuing of this declaration, on top of all of the king's other "adjustments," rattled the Anglican and Protestant clergymen. Their initial shock turned to bubbling bitterness when James ordered for these sacrilegious declarations to be read out from every pulpit in every church, or the "Order in Council." Blood pressures were spiking across the land.

To discuss the situation, the Archbishop of Canterbury, William Sancroft, invited 6 bishops to a private supper party in the borough of Lambeth in Central London. Grievances were laid out on the table, and solutions tossed around. By the time the last crumb had been licked from its plate, 7 of the clergymen signed a formal petition to denounce the Declaration of Indulgence. The petition claimed that the declaration was considered illegal under traditional Parliament law and should remain that way, as it threatened the fabric of Protestant English principles.

Sancroft

Sancroft himself had been the one to crown James, but now even he had come to his breaking point. The stark shift was staggeringly clear. On the 19th of May, the petition began to circulate in print, with anti-monarchists and rebels passing them out on the streets like last-day-sale flyers.

Out of the 100 or so churches in all of London, only 4 of these were said to have abided by the Order in Council.

One can only imagine how incensed the king must have been when word finally reached him. Almost at once, James slammed his foot down and had these bishops tried by a court of law under the charge of "seditious libel." During the trial, the bishops, under advice from their lawyers, kept a cool head. They would not admit to creating the petition, but would not withdraw from it, either. All throughout the trials, they calmly maintained that they had done nothing wrong. At every recess of their trials, they were greeted by hordes of supporters. Hundreds cheered the bishops on as they were being marched up and down the stairs of Whitehall. People, even nobles, waded through dirt and mud that reached their waists, all in the hopes of getting a quick blessing from the bishops. Many of these soldiers who were asked to guard the prisoners had also become enamored of them, and treated them with great respect. Eventually, the bishops were acquitted by the jury. The ecstatic crowds that gladly received them tripled in size.

Some of the bishops' supporters were the very nonconformists the king set out to free, but many saw the indulgence as a despicable act of bribery, aiming to destroy all the good that had been brought by the Reformation. One of James's loudest opponents was the dissenter and author of *Robinson Crusoe*, Daniel Defoe. A young Defoe was said to have declared, "I had rather the Church of England should pull our clothes off by fines and forfeitures, than the Papists should fall both upon the Church and the Dissenters, and pull our skins off by fire and faggott."

Defoe

Rumors, Conspiracy, and the Final Straw

"God be thanked we were not bred up in that communion but are of a Church that is pious and sincere, and conformable in all its principles to the Scriptures...the Church of England is, without all doubt, the only true Church." – Excerpt from a letter Princess Anne wrote to Mary, 1686

James's second wife, Mary of Modena, was as fertile as can be, but her children either perished in the womb or had their lives cut short by disease. Unwilling to give up, James and his wife tried just about every fertility treatment available at the time, even consuming wine mixed with hare spittle, floating bits of mice ears, bay-berries, eggs, and other roots and herbs. While these treatments might seem downright bizarre today, these practices were embraced by women and many medical experts of the time.

Something must have worked, because in fall of 1677, a delighted Mary of Modena announced that she was with child. In the early hours of June 10, 1688, a shrieking Mary doubled over in pain, feeling the blistering pains of labor contractions. Palace staff hastened to the royal bedchambers in clusters, watching anxiously by the door. As painful as it was, the labor only lasted a few hours, and by 10:00 a.m., the wailing baby had been born.

James and Mary were over the moon. After years and years of trial and error, they had finally produced a baby boy. They named him after the king, and from then on, the new prince was known as James Francis Edward. For weeks, doctors kept a close eye on the infant, feeding him postnatal gruel made of flour, water, sugar, and a splash of white wine, as well as milk from a wet nurse. James Francis was the picture of health – chubby, cherry-red cheeks, twinkling eyes, and a full head of thick, sandy-gold hair.

James Francis

The tidings of a healthy newborn are typically met with warm congratulations and jovial celebration, but with the introduction of James Francis, the Protestants were in uproar. As a matter of fact, James's very own children from his first marriage, Mary and Anne, wrinkled their noses at the news. Before James Francis, Mary and Anne had been the most likely candidates to succeed the throne, but this new male heir had set all their plans of reverting to a Protestant England ablaze. James Francis would undoubtedly be raised Catholic, thereby prolonging the dreaded Catholic rule.

This was when the rumors started pouring in, and James would see his own flesh and blood turn against him. Mary and Anne had never gotten along with their stepmother, Mary of Modena, who was only 4 years older than Mary, and with their new half-brother now on the scene, the sisters hatred for their stepmother only deepened. At the time, James's second daughter still resided in the palace, where she lived with her husband, Prince George of Denmark. Anne was the first to question the supposedly ill-fitting pieces to the puzzle, and began to question the circumstances surrounding the mysterious birth. For example, she wondered how Mary seemed to have recovered so quickly after childbirth, when during past births she would be bedridden for sometimes weeks at a time. Furthermore, she claimed that James had been far too confident about the gender of his child, almost as if he were certain of it, which was impossible in an age before ultrasounds. On top of that, some claimed that the baby boy had been smuggled into the queen's bed in a warming pan (an apparatus that resembles a frying pan with a lid on it; filled with coals and placed under beds). In other words, it was concluded that this boy was a "changeling."

Then came another rumor. Word on the street was that Mary of Modena had actually been adopted by the Duke of Modena, and that she was actually the secret daughter of Pope Clement X. Apparently, in 1673, young Mary had been convicted of a crime and was on the verge of being buried alive when Pope Clement came to her rescue. In exchange for her freedom, he instructed her to marry the Duke of York, securing their plan of Catholic domination in place.

Another tale was spun about the baby prince, who many mocked as the "Warming Pan Prince of Wales." Some suspected that his real father was Richard Talbot, Earl of Tyrconnell and Lord Lieutenant to James. His "real" mother is known only as an Irish woman named "Mrs. Gray." After the baby was taken from her, Mrs. Gray was shipped off to a secluded convent in Paris. She would later escape from the convent and attempt to locate her baby, only to be intercepted by Jesuits and promptly killed.

The propaganda against Prince James was stamped on thousands of pamphlets and hawked left and right. In spite of the documented 70 witnesses who were present during the birth, Princess Anne either firmly believed or chose to believe these tall tales. Mary, who was in the Netherlands, had also received word about the new addition to the family and began to exchange letters with her sister, sending long lists of questions and requesting regular updates. The sisters stroked their chins. Something just wasn't right.

Mary's husband would also begin to grow suspicious over his father-in-law's true motives. After all, he too, as James' son-in-law, was also in the running for the throne, something he believed that King Charles II, who had arranged his marriage with Mary, had intended. But whatever William suspected about the baby, he kept his opinions to himself.

Though James had initially opposed William and Mary's marriage, his relationship with his son-in-law enjoyed a promising start. During the Monmouth Rebellion, William had even sent Dutch mercenaries to England to help the struggling king.

Once James was crowned, however, their relationship began to strain. William began to grow suspicious of James, often questioning him about the king's ties to France. William reckoned that

James had forged a secret alliance with King Louis XIV, as James's military tactics and Catholic vision seemed greatly reminiscent of the French king. Even more suspicious, James would not return the favor when William asked for his help with his anti-French campaigns.

Whatever the case, the pair began to distance themselves from one another, and in January of 1688, James commanded William to remove all the English and Scottish armies based in the Netherlands. When William refused, a ruddy-faced James ordered all his men to simply desert William's forces and return to Britain. William, who did not want the extra weight of James's supporters dragging him down, swiftly agreed and bid them good riddance.

As another example, when James began his mission to repeal the Test Acts, he sought help from his son-in-law in Hague, but William would not bite, not even when William Penn was sent to the Hague on behalf of James. William opted to stay out of it, stating that he gave his full support to the Church of England. James would try again and again, assuring William that none of the rumors about his ties with the French were true. Still, William would not budge. He advised James to stick to the law and warned him that all these changes he was making would one day come back to haunt him. The equally stubborn James shrugged off William's many warnings.

William Penn

The Plotting Begins

"Every bullet has its billet." – William III of Orange

Historians believe it was Mary who first planted the idea of an English invasion in William's mind to depose James, which meant betraying her own father. But this was worth it to her because she believed the future of Protestant England was at stake.

Even so, an initially hesitant William would need a little more coaxing from his wife, because William's approval of the plan was supposedly hindered by his jealousy. He did not want to risk a second in the cold depths of her shadow; after all, if Mary was to take the throne, his wife, as the queen of England, would be more powerful than he was. It was only when an unyielding Mary convinced him that political power was the last thing on her mind that William began to shift his stance. Mary promised that she would stay by his side to the end as his wife, and "that she would do all that lay in her power to make him king for life." The pair finally agreed to an equal partnership, ruling as joint monarchs.

Some say that William had begun to plot for the invasion as early as November of 1687, when the news of Mary of Modena's pregnancy was first announced. Whether or not that is true is still up for debate, but what is known for certain is that by April of 1688, William had officially set his mind to the task. That month, William learned that King Louis and King James had signed off on a suspicious naval agreement that ensured France would provide funding for the English warships, which could only mean that James had been lying all along – the French and the English were, as he had always suspected, in cahoots.

With this in mind, the famously prudent William began to draw up plans for the invasion. He did not want to take on England without being certain that the people of England would have his back, because to do otherwise would be the move of an amateur. Indeed, the invasion would require some meticulous planning. Later that same month, William requested that a formal letter of invitation be sent to him by England's top-most politicians. A letter addressed to him by the "most valued men in the nation" showcasing their support would be the ultimate green light. If everything went as planned, he assured them that he would be ready by September.

Come May, William was greeted with bittersweet news. The rebels in England were growing antsy and did not want to wait any longer. They threatened to act now, with or without him. William was pleased to hear of their enthusiasm about putting an end to James's pro-Catholic reign, but he knew this was not the time. In fact, in early June, William sent an ambassador to James's palace to congratulate the king on his newborn son. This was allegedly just a front, because when William's agent left the palace, he secretly met with conspirators to smooth out the kinks of their plan and convinced them to hold on just a while longer to ensure a more triumphant outcome.

As rumors about Prince James Francis began to move throughout the kingdom, that letter William had been pining for arrived in the mail. He sliced off the wax seal excitedly, his heart thumping in his anticipation. His eyes settled on the signatures scrawled across the bottom of the letter – the Earl of Danby, the Earl of Shrewsbery, the Earl of Devonshire, Viscount Lumley, Admiral Edward Russell, Politician Henry Sydney, and Bishop Henry Compton – otherwise known as the "Immortal Seven." An excerpt from the letter read, "We have great reason to believe, we shall be everyday in a worse condition than we are, and less able to defend ourselves, and therefore we do earnestly wish we might be so happy as to find a remedy before it be too late for us to contribute to our own deliverance..."

Sydney

In hopes of restoring the power of the Church of England, as well as the creation of a new "free" Parliament, the Immortal Seven pledged their allegiance to William. The authors of the letter went on to declare that James had gone too far by abusing his "right of dispensation," playing puppeteer by overriding the laws of Parliament with his dreadful monarchy. The letter claimed that most officials in government were gravely discontent, and were only holding onto their jobs so that bills could be paid. The morale of the people was so low that "19 parts of 20 of the people throughout the country" all longed for change, and would give William their full support. William must have known that the statistic was a bit of an exaggeration, but nonetheless, their words were music to his ears.

In the first week of July, William Bentinck, one of William's most loyal associates, reached English soil, armed with satchels crammed with stacks of propaganda pamphlets. These pamphlets portrayed William as a knight in shining armor of sorts. The aspiring king was promoted as the best of all the Stuart candidates, and one who aimed to give the Protestant public (roughly 90% of the population) what they wanted. William swore he would ban the secret practicing of Catholicism and vowed to dismantle the tradition of absolutism, wherein the people were ruled under one monarch. He vowed to give more power to Parliament and the people. This same pamphlet also devoted a section to condemning the newborn, James Francis, who they branded the "Pretended [sic] Prince of Wales."

Thanks to Bentinck and his men, William secured most of the English public's support in less than 2 months. Even so, William was still leery of the alleged alliance between Louis and James, which would most certainly pose a problem for him in the future. More reinforcement was needed, so William sent another ambassador to the neighboring Austrian city of Vienna. His agent crept into the palace unnoticed, where he met with Holy Roman Emperor, Leopold I. A deal was struck up between both parties. William promised that by restoring Protestantism in England, he would not persecute the Catholics. If William kept up his end of the deal, Leopold would grant him a portion of his military when the time came. Lastly, Leopold agreed he would later join forces in an alliance against France.

Leopold I

The next step was to secure funding. Amsterdam was a global frontrunner in the 17th century, and the bustling financial hub of the world, making it a perfect bank of sorts. Be that as it may, actually acquiring a loan from the city would prove tougher than expected, as many of the top officials in the city were well-known supporters of the French. Thankfully for William, the French king would turn his Dutch supporters against him when he drove up tariffs and set limits on herring exports, which stung many Dutch businesses.

Eventually, 260 transports were hired. Bentinck, William's shining star, also began to drum up and negotiate contracts with mercenaries all over Europe, furthering the army expansion. By the end of Bentinck's endeavors, he had signed up over 13,500 German soldiers. The rest of William's loans came from unlikely sources. There was the Jewish banker, Francisco Suasso, who lent him a sum of 2 million guilders (approximately $200 million USD today). Suasso was supposedly so supportive that he did not ask for collateral. Taking a gamble, he told William to pay him back when he could, and if William failed to generate the funds, Suasso would simply take it as a loss. Another 4 million guilders were collected to patch up and bolster the fortresses in the east. Even Pope Innocent XI himself was said to have contributed to the funds, offering him a loan of at least 500,000 guilders. The Vatican would later deny that any such fund was provided for this purpose.

Bentinck

Suasso

Funds were also collected to pay the salaries of all the hired soldiers, along with 9,000 sailors. The ever fruitful Bentinck then traveled to the German city of Brandenburg to meet and sweet-talk the new elector. Another few thousand soldiers were added to William's disposal. By now, William and his men had amassed the following: 43 decked out and armed boats; 4 light frigates (another type of warship), and 10 "fireships" that could hold over 20,000 soldiers.

William may have garnered the support of almost all of England, but the same could not be said about his own people. No matter how hard he tried, he could not persuade his own top officials that this egregiously expensive expedition was absolutely necessary. Dutch officials were simply not swayed, and many of them feared going bankrupt. In response, one of the Immortal Seven suggested that they push the mission back a year, but William would not have it. The window of opportunity was quickly closing, and William feared they would never be able to squeeze through. At one point, these concerns had become so taxing that for a fleeting moment, William considered canceling the mission altogether.

Lo and behold, another window cracked open, and once again, it was the French king's own tempestuous temperament that made it happen. The pope refused to approve the candidate Louis had been heavily hyping for the Bishop of Cologne, which angered him so much that he decided to steer his attention towards Germany, springing to action before his French forces could be removed from the country. On September 9, 1688, the States General of the Netherlands was handed a pair of letters signed by King Louis. The first letter gruffly ordered the Dutch forces to keep away from England, and that they were not to, under any circumstances, disrupt the peace with English troops. In the second letter, the Dutch were asked not to pry their noses into the French movement in Germany. The startled Dutch general, along with his peers, were finally convinced that James was really working with the French after all. Later that week, Louis banished Dutch ships from all the ports in France.

Louis had allegedly done so to show the Dutch that he meant business, but this would blow up in his face. William reminded the Dutch officials of the horrors of 1672, when England and France had ganged up on the Netherlands. Hoping to avoid a repeat of history, the Dutch finally gave William their support on the 26th of September. James would continue to vehemently deny the allegiance, but this letter from Louis was all the proof they needed.

The Takeover

"If occasion were, I hope God would give me his grace to suffer death for the true Catholic religion as well as banishment." – King James II

William's invasion fleet was a force of nature on its own. The Dutch army was at least 20,000 strong, though many of them were foreign mercenaries, including Scots, Swiss, Germans, and English rebels. A few dozen natives and 200 black men from Dutch-owned plantations in America were also brought on board. The troops were split into 3 squadrons of warships, which were to be led by Admirals Van Almonde, Herbert, and Eversten.

Meanwhile, massive container vessels were stuffed with 11,000 horses – including William's own personal coach and stallions – as well as over 20,000 rifles, ammunition, and other weapons. Other vessels contained a printing press, a portable bridge, a mobile blacksmith workshop, and molds for minting Orange-brand currency. A wide range of provisions were stocked, nourishment aplenty. There were 1,600 casks of beer and 50 more of brandy, each carrying 64 gallons of liquor, as well as 4 tons of tobacco and 10,000 pairs of boots to appease the troops.

On October 26, 1688, the Dutch warships, with William on the flagship, set sail for England. The Dutch spent the first few days coasting along the still waters, but before the second week's end, the fleet was ensnared in the eye of a sudden storm. While none of the men were hurt, they would lose about 1,300 horses. They suffocated behind their locked hatches, which had been sealed over with planks of wood as an emergency precaution.

Once the waters had calmed, the Dutch ships set sail once more. With the help of the so-called "Protestant Wind," an auspicious gust of wind from the east that blew west, the rest of the voyage carried on smoothly. As William's flagship, the Den Briel, sailed past the small Isle of Wight, the prince received his first boost of confidence. At least 300 of the island villagers had gathered by the shore, spurring them on with spirited whoops and hollers. The awe-stricken villagers marveled at the magnificent Dutch warships, the giant streamers tethered to the posts of the gleaming vessels rippling in the wind. Each streamer bore a different message. The one on William's ship bore the classic Orange motto, "Je Maintendrai." The others shared similar Latin slogans: "Pro libertate et religone." Together, the streamers proclaimed, "The Liberty of England and the Protestant Religion, I Will Maintain."

On the 15th of November (or the 5th of November in the Old Style Calendar), William and Mary finally reached solid ground. The fleet parked themselves at the coast of the small fishing town of Brixham, near the borough of Torbay. Upon landing, a Dutch chaplain who had come along summoned the troops for a prayer session. The soldiers linked hands and sang Psalm 118, an ode of gratitude to their God.

An equestrian portrait of William commemorating his landing

William's second confidence boost came from the villagers of Brixham, who were nothing but overjoyed to see the Dutch. The prince was instantly recognized by the distinctive coat of arms on the chest of his armor. Giddy villagers surrounded him, gushing their praises. Women stooped over to kiss his hands. A fisherman was said to have even swept William off his feet, prancing around with the prince on his shoulders. That evening, the villagers opened up their homes to William and his troops. They spoiled them with a feast and provided them with shelter for the night.

3 days later, William and his army forged on to the cathedral city of Exeter, where he would meet even more of his fans. The prince was received with another round of celebrations as the congested streets, including local clergymen, toasted him and showered him with well wishes. There, the Dutch began their distribution of over 60,000 pamphlets, The Declaration of Hague. The pamphlets, which had been translated to English, reminded the people that William had arrived to free them from James' oppressive reign, along with other reiterations of his policies. The villagers would also be rewarded a glimpse of William's "fair ruling" when he had 2 of his own soldiers publicly executed after they were found guilty of swiping a chicken.

In the days that followed, William was visited by powerful English officials, including the commander at the Plymouth Garrison, who offered William a healthy fraction of his troops. From there, William's army grew even stronger. His future was looking brighter than ever, and it was only now that James realized he was under attack. While James possessed a combined army of over 34,000 men, the majority of these soldiers were Protestants who would soon desert him. Before he could even summon his armies, the revolts had already begun, beginning with one in Cheshire County. He strove to stamp out William's forces, but he was met with one failure after another. Gradually, more and more of his generals began to abandon him to join William.

The deflated English king was swiftly losing steam. The warm reception and hospitality his own people showed his son-in-law further disconcerted him. All the stress had also triggered a series of nosebleeds, which James considered yet another black omen. There was no denying it: the end seemed near.

On the 7th of December, William and James' representatives convened at the Bear Inn in the town of Hungerford. William's smug agents slid a document across the table, which listed the prince's terms. The terms were: the dismissal of all Catholic officers, effective immediately; to retract all ill statements made against William and his party; for James to reimburse William for all the military costs of the expedition; and a promise from James that he would not seek help from French troops.

William promoted a peaceful resolution to end all of the drama. He agreed to keep his army at bay, 40 miles west of London, if and only if James promised to do the same, but 40 miles to the east. In his terms, William showed no signs of his intentions to take over the throne. Instead, he appeared almost merciful and open to compromise with his father-in-law. James would be allowed to keep his crown, but his powers would considerably shrink.

James received the terms the next evening, and assured William's agents that they would receive an answer the morning after. But the king had other plans. At this point, his wife, dressed as a laundrywoman, had already taken their child and escaped to France. James decided that he, too, would join them. On the night of December 11th, James set sail for France, accompanied by 2 Catholic comrades. As they sailed through the dark waters, James flung the "Great Seal of the Realm," the sovereign's official wax seal, over the side of the ship. Many saw this as a symbolic gesture of James's breakup with England.

James, a magnet for misfortune, would not go very far. Just 4 days later, he was apprehended by a pair of Kentish fishermen, towed back to English shore, and thrown into a cell. The disgraced king, who had now earned himself the unflattering nickname "Dismal Jimmy," would be locked behind bars for several days as the people called for his execution. In a final show of mercy, William allowed James to leave. And that he did. 2 days before Christmas, James left for England, never to return again.

The Joint Monarchs

"There is one certain means by which I can be sure never to see my country's ruin: I will die in the last ditch." – William III of Orange

With James gone, a unanimous decision was made by the House of Lords. They declared that King James had deserted his throne and was therefore stripped of his royal title. A week later, the crown was tendered to William and Mary, under the stipulation that Mary remain childless. At this juncture, Mary had been diagnosed with a critical illness and was now barren, so there was no need to think twice.

Though this stipulation was directed at Mary, it was no secret that William was in the driver's seat, and his wife, while sitting up front with him, was simply a passenger. The division of power was clear. The House of Lords would oversee civil administration, whereas William and Mary would have full control of the military. On the 29th of December, the pair were put in charge of the temporary government.

For Mary, this victory had come with a price. A part of her was conflicted for having betrayed her own father, but at the end of the day, there had been no other alternative. Freedom from James's incompetence and disorderly reign, Mary believed, was for the good of the people. It was what they needed and what they deserved.

In February of 1689, Mary finally reunited with her husband in Greenwich. That month, Parliament, along with the Tories and the Whigs, gathered to create the "Declaration of Rights." This document would later be amended and given a new title – the "Bill of Rights." The bill listed in detail the terms and regulations the monarchs-to-be were to abide by if they were to be given the crown. First and foremost, Parliament was to schedule regular meetings more frequently. The Parliament would essentially hold more power. The monarchs were not allowed to interfere with the selection of Parliament members, but possessed the right to veto bills and may pardon whoever they choose to. The monarchs were not permitted a standing army or embark on any military campaigns without Parliament's consent.

The bill would also protect the English people. Freedom of speech would be guaranteed to all. Unhappy citizens, no matter what creed, were free to petition for whatever cause they pleased. A Toleration Act was later passed so that no more would be compelled to join the Church of England. That said, Protestant nonconformists and other dissenters were still made to shell out a tenth of their annual earnings to the Church of England, which were taxes known as "tithes."

Moreover, the monarchs would no longer hold the right to determine the religion of his or her subjects, as religion was now separate from politics. Kings and queens must now accept that they were second to Parliament in power, and the policy of the "Divine Right of Kings" was officially extinct. England was now a true constitutional monarchy. This new government formed the foundations of the modern British Parliament.

Britain's first and only coronation for joint sovereigns was set for April 11, 1689. This was William and Mary's special day, and the exuberance that had overcome the public was infectious, but clearly not everyone was in the mood for celebrating. That morning, Mary received a strongly-worded letter from James. He reproached her, "The curses of an angry father will fall on you, as well as those of a God who commands obedience to his parents." With a heavy heart, Mary crumpled up the letter and chucked it aside, determined not to let anything put a damper on her day. William and Mary appeared at Westminster Abbey, where the Declaration of Rights was read to them once more. Once the pair had agreed, they were crowned by Henry Compton, the Bishop of London.

Compton

After a 3-hour ceremony, the new monarchs emerged from behind the glossy timber doors. The couple strode down the stairs, their ceremonial robes swishing majestically around their feet. Sporting a lustrous bejeweled crown with a velvet bonnet, King William waved at the whistling congregation in front of him. Next to him stood Queen Mary in a twinkling tiara, with her beaming face immaculately painted, radiating pride. The husband and wife would later enjoy a lovely banquet, with festivities lasting until 10 in the evening.

The striking saga of the Glorious Revolution is one that continues to fascinate historians around the world today. Some chroniclers have referred to these events as the "Bloodless Revolution," but other historians say otherwise. The ruthless game of politics that William and James played may have been somewhat bloodless in comparison to history's greatest rebellions, but the rebels, soldiers, and other pawns who lost their lives along the way must not be forgotten. The revolution would also pave the path for a series of bloody wars between England and Scotland, the result of which has left quite a legacy of its own.

Online Resources

Other books about English history by Charles River Editors

Other books about the Glorious Revolution on Amazon

Bibliography

1.   Vallance, Edward, PhD. "The Glorious Revolution." BBC . BBC, 17 Feb. 2011. Web. 16 Jan. 2017. <http://www.bbc.co.uk/history/british/civil_war_revolution/glorious_revolution_01.shtml>.

2.   Handlin, Emily. "The History of the Coronation of James II." Brown University Library. History of Art and Architecture Department, 2012. Web. 16 Jan. 2017. <http://library.brown.edu/readingritual/handlin_jamesII.html>.

3.   Knowles, Rachel. "The Whigs and the Tories." Regency History. Blogger, 21 Apr. 2015. Web. 16 Jan. 2017. <http://www.regencyhistory.net/2015/04/the-whigs-and-tories.html>.

4.   Trueman, C. N. "The 1688 Revolution." The History Learning Site. The History Learning Site, Ltd., 16 Aug. 2016. Web. 16 Jan. 2017. <http://www.historylearningsite.co.uk/stuart-england/the-1688-revolution/>.

5.   Trueman, C. N. "The Popish Plot." The History Learning Site. The History Learning Site, Ltd., 17 Mar. 2015. Web. 16 Jan. 2017. <http://www.historylearningsite.co.uk/stuart-england/the-popish-plot/>.

6.   Rennell, Tony. "The 1688 invasion of Britain that's been erased from history." The Daily Mail. Associated Newspapers, Ltd., 18 Apr. 2008. Web. 16 Jan. 2017. <http://www.dailymail.co.uk/news/article-560614/The-1688-invasion-Britain-thats-erased-history.html>.

7.   Stocker, Barry. "The Glorious Revolution and the Immortal 7's Letter." Bosphorus Reflections: Barry Stocker's Weblog. Blogger, 2 July 2009. Web. 16 Jan. 2017. <http://www.bbc.co.uk/history/people/william_iii_of_orange>.

8.   Jonathan. "Great Events in British History: William of Orange and the Glorious Revolution." Anglotopia. Anglotopia, LLC, 8 June 2015. Web. 16 Jan. 2017. <http://www.anglotopia.net/british-history/great-events-in-british-history-william-of-orange-and-the-glorious-revolution/>.

9.   Editors, Britannia. "William III and Mary II (1689-1702 AD)." Britannia. Britannia, LLC, 2012. Web. 16 Jan. 2017. <http://www.britannia.com/history/monarchs/mon51.html>.

10.   Heathcoate, John. "Pope cut out of Orange history." FantomPowa. N.p., 1998. Web. 16 Jan. 2017. <http://www.fantompowa.net/Flame/pope_cut_out_of_.htm>.

11.   Editors, CRF. "England's Glorious Revolution." Constitutional Rights Foundation. Constitutional Rights Foundation, 2017. Web. 16 Jan. 2017. <http://www.crf-usa.org/bill-of-rights-in-action/bria-25-3-england-glorious-revolution.html>.

12.   Editors, SMLOL. "The Glorious Revolution of 1688." THE SOMME MEMORIAL LOYAL ORANGE LODGE 842. THE SOMME MEMORIAL LOYAL ORANGE LODGE, 2009. Web. 16 Jan. 2017. <http://www.lol842bristol.com/index.php?p=1_36_Glorious-Revolution>.

13.   Admin, HIH. "England and the Popish Plot." History in an Hour. WordPress, 17 Oct. 2010. Web. 16 Jan. 2017. <http://www.historyinanhour.com/2010/10/17/england-and-the-popish-plot/>.

14.   Petty, Mike. "The Classic Sir Edmund Berry Godfrey Coincidence Which Isn't Quite What It Appears." 67 Not Out. Blogger, 16 Aug. 2013. Web. 16 Jan. 2017. <http://www.67notout.com/2013/08/the-classic-sir-edmund-berry-godfrey.html>.

15.   Editors, History Channel. "Enlightenment." History Channel. A&E Television Networks, LLC, 2016. Web. 16 Jan. 2017. <http://www.history.com/topics/enlightenment>.

16.   Editors, SparkNotes. "THE ENLIGHTENMENT (1650–1800)." SparkNotes. SparkNotes, LLC, 2015. Web. 16 Jan. 2017. <http://www.sparknotes.com/history/european/enlightenment/terms.html>.

17.   Editors, Kepler College. "Francis Bacon: The Natural Philosopher." Kepler College. Kepler College, 2015. Web. 16 Jan. 2017. <http://www.kepler.edu/home/index.php/articles/history-of-astrology/item/333-francis-bacon-the-natural-philosopher>.

18.   Editors, Biography Online. "John Locke biography." Biography Online. Biography Online, 2014. Web. 16 Jan. 2017. <http://www.biographyonline.net/writers/john-locke-biography.html>.

19.   Brom, Robert H. "Papal Infallibility." Catholic Answers. Catholic Answers, 10 Aug. 2004. Web. 16 Jan. 2017. <https://www.catholic.com/tract/papal-infallibility>.

20.   Morris, Marc. "King John: the most evil monarch in Britain's history." The Telegraph. Telegraph Media Group, Ltd., 13 June 2015. Web. 16 Jan. 2017. <http://www.telegraph.co.uk/culture/11671441/King-John-the-most-evil-monarch-in-Britains-history.html>.

21.　Nix, Elizabeth. "8 Things You Might Not Know about Mary I." History Channel. A&E Television Networks, LLC, 16 Feb. 2016. Web. 16 Jan. 2017. <http://www.history.com/news/8-things-you-might-not-know-about-mary-i>.

22.　Trueman, C. N. "Louis XIV and religion." The History Learning Site. The History Learning Site, Ltd., 17 Mar. 2015. Web. 16 Jan. 2017. <http://www.historylearningsite.co.uk/france-in-the-seventeenth-century/louis-xiv-and-religion/>.

23.　Editors, History Channel. "Great Fire of London begins." History Channel. A&E Television Networks, LLC, 2 Sept. 2015. Web. 16 Jan. 2017. <http://www.history.com/this-day-in-history/great-fire-of-london-begins>.

24.　Shimmin, Graeme. "Are there any conspiracy theories behind the Great Fire of London?" Quora. Quora, Inc., 19 Dec. 2013. Web. 16 Jan. 2017. <https://www.quora.com/Are-there-any-conspiracy-theories-behind-the-Great-Fire-of-London>.

25.　McRobbie, Linda Rodriguez. "The Great Fire of London Was Blamed on Religious Terrorism." The Smithsonian Magazine. The Smithsonian Institution, 2 Sept. 2016. Web. 17 Jan. 2017. <http://www.smithsonianmag.com/history/great-fire-london-was-blamed-religious-terrorism-180960332/>.

26.　Porter, Margaret. "A Coronation Feast, 23 April, 1685." English Historical Fiction Authors. Blogspot, 23 Feb. 2015. Web. 17 Jan. 2017. <http://englishhistoryauthors.blogspot.tw/2015/02/a-coronation-feast-23-april-1685.html>.

27.　Editors, Encyclopedia.Com. "James II (King Of England, Scotland, And Ireland)." Encyclopedia.Com. The Columbia University Press, 2014. Web. 17 Jan. 2017. <http://www.encyclopedia.com/people/history/british-and-irish-history-biographies/james-ii-england>.

28.　Editors, History Channel. "King Charles I executed for treason." History Channel. A&E Television Networks, LLC, 30 Jan. 2015. Web. 17 Jan. 2017. <http://www.history.com/this-day-in-history/king-charles-i-executed-for-treason>.

29.　Editors, Scandalous Women. "Royal Mistresses: Catherine Sedley, Countess of Dorchester." Scandalous Women. Blogspot, 27 Aug. 2008. Web. 17 Jan. 2017. <http://scandalouswoman.blogspot.tw/2008/08/royal-mistresses-catherine-sedley.html>.

30.　Derrick, Kiri. "Top 10 Philandering English Monarchs." Listverse. Listverse, Ltd., 21 Apr. 2011. Web. 17 Jan. 2017. <http://listverse.com/2011/04/21/top-10-philandering-english-monarchs/>.

31. Editors, Parliament UK. "Whigs and Tories." Parliament UK. Parliament UK, 2015. Web. 17 Jan. 2017. <http://www.parliament.uk/about/living-heritage/evolutionofparliament/parliamentaryauthority/revolution/overview/whigstories/>.

32. Editors, Parliament UK. "Catholics and Protestants." Parliament UK. Parliament UK, 2015. Web. 17 Jan. 2017. <http://www.parliament.uk/about/living-heritage/evolutionofparliament/parliamentaryauthority/revolution/overview/catholicsprotestants/>.

33. Editors, Your Dictionary. "William III Facts." Your Dictionary. Love To Know Corporation, 2013. Web. 17 Jan. 2017. <http://biography.yourdictionary.com/william-iii>.

34. Editors, Encyclopedia.Com. "Mary II." Encyclopedia.Com. The Gale Group, Inc., 2015. Web. 17 Jan. 2017. <http://www.encyclopedia.com/people/history/british-and-irish-history-biographies/mary-ii>.

35. Editors, English Monarch. "William III and Mary II." English Monarchs. English Monarchs, 2005. Web. 17 Jan. 2017. <http://www.englishmonarchs.co.uk/stuart_6.htm>.

36. Lucy, Gordon. "Share: The Legacy Of William Of Orange." The Orange Order. Grand Orange Lodge of Ireland, 2012. Web. 17 Jan. 2017. <http://www.grandorangelodge.co.uk/history.aspx?id=99484#.WIGpH_l95EZ>.

37. Dennison, Matthew. "The merry monarch and his mistresses; was sex for Charles II a dangerous distraction?" The Spectator. The Spectator, Ltd., 31 Jan. 2015. Web. 17 Jan. 2017. <http://www.spectator.co.uk/2015/01/the-merry-monarch-and-his-mistresses-was-sex-for-charles-ii-a-dangerous-distraction/>.

38. "First Inaugural Address of Abraham Lincoln." The Avalon Project. Lillian Goldman Law Library, 2008. Web. 17 Jan. 2017. <http://avalon.law.yale.edu/19th_century/lincoln1.asp>.

39. Editors, The Reformation. "The Rye House Plot 1683." The Reformation. WordPress, 12 Mar. 2016. Web. 17 Jan. 2017. <http://www.thereformation.info/rye_house_plot.htm>.

40. Editors, GMMG. "THE LAST SLEEP OF THE EARL OF ARGYLL." Greater Manchester Museum Group. Greater Manchester Museum Group, 2013. Web. 17 Jan. 2017. <http://www.gmmg.org.uk/our-connected-history/item/last-sleep-of-argyll/>.

41. Editors, HH. "Dame Alice Lisle." Hampshire History. Hampshire History, 28 Oct. 2013. Web. 18 Jan. 2017. <http://www.hampshire-history.com/dame-alice-lisle/>.

42.   Editors, New World Encyclopedia. "James II of England." New World Encylopedia. MediaWiki, 27 Apr. 2014. Web. 18 Jan. 2017. <http://www.newworldencyclopedia.org/entry/James_II_of_England>.

43.   Campbell, K. K. "King Louis XIV: French Mastermind." History Net. World History Group, 12 June 2006. Web. 18 Jan. 2017. <http://www.historynet.com/king-louis-xiv-french-mastermind.htm>.

44.   Editors, Spanish Succession. "The English Army." Spanish Succession. N.p., 2015. Web. 18 Jan. 2017. <http://www.spanishsuccession.nl/english_army.html#3>.

45.   McFerran, Noel S. "Declaration of Indulgence of King James II, April 4, 1687." The Jacobite Heritage. Noel McFerran, 25 Oct. 2003. Web. 18 Jan. 2017. <http://www.jacobite.ca/documents/16870404.htm>.

46.   Scrivener, Patrick. "THE WARMING PAN PRINCE OF WALES PLOT EXPOSED AT LAST!!" Reformation.Org. Patrick Scrivener, 2016. Web. 18 Jan. 2017. <http://www.reformation.org/warming-pan-prince-of-wales-plot-exposed.html>.

47.   Taylor, Jerome. "When 17th-century women would seek out hare spittle." The Independent. Associated Newspapers, Ltd., 29 Nov. 2007. Web. 18 Jan. 2017. <http://www.independent.co.uk/life-style/health-and-families/features/when-17th-century-women-would-seek-out-hare-spittle-760836.html>.

48.   Smitha, Frank E. "William and Mary, a Glorious Revolution and Bill of Rights." Macro History and World Timeline. Frank E Smitha, 2015. Web. 18 Jan. 2017. <http://www.fsmitha.com/h3/h25eng5.htm>.

49.   Childs, John. Army, James II and the Glorious Revolution. N.p.: Manchester U Press, 1980. Print.

50.   Craik, George Lillie. The Pictorial History of England During the Reign of George the Third. Vol. 3. N.p.: RareClub.com, 2012. Print.

51.   Aubrey, John. Aubrey's Brief Lives. N.p.: Nonpareil , 2015. Print.

52.   Instructor, The Catholic. The Catholic Instructor. Vol. 3. N.p.: RareClub.com, 2012. Print.

53.   Alexander, Rachel. Myths, Symbols and Legends of Solar System Bodies (The Patrick Moore Practical Astronomy Series). N.p.: Springer, 2015. Print.

54.   Crompton, Louis. Homosexuality and Civilization. N.p.: Belknap Press, 2006. Print.

55. Starkey, David. "The Glorious Revolution." Monarchy with David Starkey. Dir. James Burge. BBC. 20 Nov. 2006. Television.

Free Books by Charles River Editors

We have brand new titles available for free most days of the week. To see which of our titles are currently free, <u>click on this link</u>.

Discounted Books by Charles River Editors

We have titles at a discount price of just 99 cents everyday. To see which of our titles are currently 99 cents, click on this link.

Made in the USA
Columbia, SC
13 August 2023

21562775R00030